GEMS AND JEWELRY IN COLOR

GEMS
AND
JEWELRY
in color

Ove Dragsted F.G.A.

Illustrated by Otto Frello

MACMILLAN PUBLISHING CO., INC.
New York

© 1975 Blandford Press
World Copyright © 1972 Politikens Forlag A/S,
Copenhagen, Denmark

MACMILLAN PUBLISHING CO., INC.
866 Third Avenue, New York, N.Y. 10022

Library of Congress Cataloging in Publication Data
Dragsted, Ove.
Gems and jewelry in color.
1. Precious stones.   2. Jewelry. I. Title.
TS752.D7 1975   736'.2   75–2391
ISBN 0–02–533500–6

First American Edition 1975

Printed in Great Britain

CONTENTS

ACKNOWLEDGEMENTS

The publishers are grateful to Mr Robert Crowningshield and Dr D. A. Robson for their valuable assistance in the preparation of this book.

INTRODUCTION

Gems are exquisite products of the animal, vegetable and mineral kingdoms wrought by man into adornments for himself and his possessions. Gems have played a large part in man's superstitions and folklore, but despite this, fashion and tastes do change, so that gems once coveted may well seem unattractive to later generations.

Now, in the twentieth century, there is an exceptionally wide range of mineral and organic gem material; new minerals and new varieties are constantly being discovered, and designers have extended the concept of jewels, using a richer variety of crystalline structures and employing new techniques to polish and fashion stones never before regarded as gems. Like the craftsmen of ancient cultures, contemporary jewellers create ornaments from snail-shells and fossils, from wood and fruits, and they set conventional stones in imaginative, new and sophisticated ways.

A precious stone is innately beautiful and its value as a gem or jewel lies in the appeal of this beauty. Some specialists, however, would restrict the term 'precious stone' to transparent stones or those of a particular hardness. Logically, *all* gems are precious stones. A precious stone is by definition genuine, produced naturally and without human intervention. By contrast man-made 'stones', not being genuine, are termed synthetic or artificial.

Stone-like structures, such as bezoar, may be derived from animals, while the seeds of some fruits, such as apricot and cherry, are also called stones. However, the word 'stone' is used predominantly for minerals and rocks.

A mineral is a natural, inorganic substance with a reasonably definite chemical composition. Its structure is usually crystalline. The atoms form a regular pattern, the atomic lattice, which determines the external geometric form of the crystal.

A rock is a part of the earth's crust and consists of one or several mineral species, or of non-crystalline mineral material. Thus lapis lazuli consists of lazurite, sodalite, noselite, hauyn and occasionally calcite and pyrite. Obsidian, a glass formed from lava, is also a rock but it has no fixed chemical composition, unlike limestone which consists of the mineral calcite.

A non-crystalline mineral with an irregular atomic structure is termed *amorphous* (Greek: formless). Crystalline minerals may lose their structure from radioactivity and amorphous glass results. The crystalline structure also disintegrates when a solid is transformed into a liquid or a gas. Strictly, perhaps, amorphous materials should not be regarded as solids, but as viscous materials, since they have not crystallised. The atoms in amorphous materials float until they have attracted and stabilised one another in a regular geometric pattern, eventually to form one or more crystals.

Organic ornamental materials may be vegetable (wood) or animal (horn, bone), and these can be transformed into minerals by fossilisation.

1 *THE ORIGIN OF GEMS AND ROCKS*

Of all the substances which appear on the earth's surface, whether associated with volcanoes, whether occurring in river valleys or on the world's beaches, gems have always proved of the greatest fascination to mankind. Long before there was any scientific body of knowledge to account for the origin of the rocks which form the earth's crust, men had evolved fantastic theories to explain the existence of gems. Diamonds, it was said, were nourished in the brains of dragons while other, less valuable jewels might be found in toads' heads. Some precious stones were thought to have fallen from the heavens. It was only when the origin of the rocks of the crust had been satisfactorily explained, less than two hundred years ago, that the true nature of gems became known.

By the third decade of the last century, it had become established that all rocks could be classified either as igneous, sedimentary or metamorphic. The igneous rocks are derived in the molten state, from the interior of the earth. The sedimentary rocks are formed from the compacted and naturally-cemented debris left by rivers, glaciers, the wind and the sea; from the accumulation of animal or vegetable remains, or from the precipitation of chemicals from the oceans. The metamorphic rocks are derived chiefly from the sedimentary rocks, by the action of heat or pressure, or both.

Igneous Rocks

The molten material within and beneath the earth's crust is described as magma. The magma, under enormous pressure, is sometimes forced up from the depths into the rocks of the crust, where it solidifies. These bodies of consolidated magma range from 100 kilometres in diameter, when they are termed batholiths, to less than one kilometre. The smaller bodies, up to about ten kilometres in diameter, are described as stocks. Batholiths and stocks, and other, similar bodies, are collectively known as major intrusions. However, the magma may be confined to injections up narrow, vertical fissures in the crust, known as dykes; or it

may be forced between the bedding planes of sedimentary rocks in the form of sills. These smaller masses of once-molten magma are described as minor intrusions.

Under certain conditions, the magma may be forced right through the crust on to the surface as a lava flow from a central crater; or it may explode from such a crater with great violence to form loose deposits of fragments, referred to as pyroclast. Whatever the form, the material which reaches the surface from the depths is described as extrusive rock. As soon as the lava is poured out on to the land, pressure on it is reduced and gases escape from its surface, leaving small cavities or vesicles in the topmost layers of the now viscous molten rock. A lava flow in which vesicles are abundant and packed close to one another is known as pumice. Vesicles generally become filled with precipitated chemicals, and are then termed amygdales; such material includes banded agate, amethyst, citrine, rock crystal, smoky quartz and morion. Sometimes a lava flow, poured out on the surface, may cool so rapidly that a glass is formed, known as obsidian; occasionally this contains minute crystals, spherulites, and the rock is described as snow-flake obsidian (99). Large crystals, or phenocrysts, which have formed before the lava reached the surface – including leucite (267) or sodalite (216) – may occur within the obsidian.

It is a law in physics that slow cooling promotes crystallisation; hence the major intrusions, cooling slowly, are coarse-grained, while the minor intrusions are medium- to fine-grained. Extrusives tend to be either fine-grained or glassy. But igneous rocks are classified not only by their mode of occurrence and grain size, but also by their chemical composition.

A silica-rich batholith or stock (over 65% silica) is described as granite, while one poor in silica is termed gabbro (45–55% silica) or peridotite (under 45% silica). Diorites and syenites lie between these extremes (55–65% silica). Diamonds occur in a special variety of peridotite known as kimberlite (124). Among the extrusive rocks, rhyolite corresponds in chemical composition to granite, andesite to diorite and basalt to gabbro.

Certain veins, known as pegmatites, are derived as vaporous offshoots from a batholith or a stock. They are coarsely crystalline and, in addition to quartz, feldspar and mica, they often contain beryl, topaz, tourmaline, garnet, apatite, spodumene and chrysoberyl. At the lower temperature and pressure found higher up, the rising vapours will produce gangues of minerals and ore with gold, platinum and rare earths.

Sedimentary Rocks

The sedimentary rocks which are most likely to yield precious stones are gravels and sands derived from some ancient land-mass which has itself been rich in gemstones. When a river brings down material from higher ground towards the sea, the movement of water provides a winnowing action which separates the heavy from the light material; therefore, pockets of denser minerals, including diamonds and nuggets of platinum and gold may occur. These are known as placer deposits.

Placer deposits may be found in ancient river deposits, for centuries consolidated into sandstones, as well as in modern fluviatile accumulations. Shore gravels, such as those in Sri Lanka, may also contain precious stones.

Layers of sedimentary rocks, being more porous than igneous formations, may become subject to intense chemical alteration through the action of percolating solutions, yielding such products as malachite, azurite, and turquoise.

Metamorphic Rocks

When a batholith or stock is emplaced within a body of sedimentary rock, e.g. shale or limestone, the heat causes a chemical reaction, with the development of minerals such as axinite, andalusite, cordierite, vesuvianite, scapolite and sphene. The process is described as contact metamorphism. Furthermore, when sedimentary rocks are subjected to intense pressures, so that the strata are folded and deformed, this also stimulates chemical changes. This is again especially the case with shales, which become transformed, with increasing pressure, into slates, phyllites and schists. A whole range of minerals is produced in association with this process, which is known as regional metamorphism, and gems like spinel, chrysoberyl, corundum, rutile, garnet, epidote, kyanite, staurolite and tourmaline are common.

2 THE EARTH'S HISTORY

However the planet earth was formed, its age has been established by radioactive measurements to be considerably more than 4,000 million years.

The long intervals of time during which the rocks of the earth's crust were laid down are described as eras. In the most ancient era, known as the Archaeozoic, the earth was devoid of life, so far as is known. This was followed by the Proterozoic, and here there is evidence of the occurrence of some forms of soft-bodied creatures. The Palaeozoic, Mesozoic, Cainozoic and Quaternary eras followed one another in turn, and throughout the 600 million years since the beginning of Palaeozoic times, the rocks contain recognisable fossil remains. In the Lower Palaeozoic era, all life was confined to the sea and was mainly invertebrate; in the Upper Palaeozoic, amphibians and land reptiles began to appear, and plant growth became luxurious. The early Mesozoic era was characterised by the emergence of enormous reptiles, dinosaurs, as well as birds. Late Mesozoic and Cainozoic times witnessed the flourishing of the mammals and the dying-out of the large reptiles. Grasses also appeared, as did the ancestors of many creatures living at the present time. The Quaternary era, spanning the most recent two million years of the earth's history, was marked by the onset of the Ice Age. Man also appeared on the scene during this time.

The formation of mineral deposits was not confined to any one era of the earth's history. For example, vast deposits of iron ore are found in the most ancient rocks of Canada, Greenland and Scandinavia; while diamonds, among other precious stones, occur in the ancient rocks of India, Brazil, and West Africa. In fact, rocks of any age may contain rich deposits of mineral ores, with their associated gemstones.

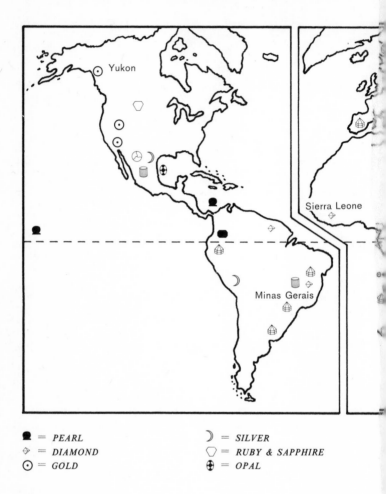

♠ = PEARL	☽ = SILVER
◇ = DIAMOND	⬠ = RUBY & SAPPHIRE
⊙ = GOLD	⊕ = OPAL

The above map indicates some of the most important deposits of precious stones. Concentrated deposits of nearly all precious stones are found in South America, in Central and Southern Africa, Madagascar and Sri Lanka (Ceylon), India, South-East Asia and Australia. Diamonds are found mainly in South America, Africa, India, Siberia and Australia.

Kashmir

Mogok

Ceylon

rley

= TOPAZ   = TURQUOISE

= EMERALD   = QUARTZ

= AMBER

3 CRYSTALS

Most minerals, and therefore gems, occur naturally as crystals. Crystals are geometrical forms. Gems are among the most beautiful of all crystals. Crystal faces are generally flat, that is plane. Adjacent faces join to form edges. The angles between faces – the interfacial angles – are constant for a crystal having a particular composition and atomic structure. In nature, even though one face may develop at the expense of another, the law of the constancy of interfacial angles remains true, though the ideal form, with each face fully developed, is rare.

Octahedral form of a crystal: (Top) *The ideal form in which the faces form angles of 120° – exactly the same as in the distorted form* (below).

Crystal Symmetry

Crystals possess symmetry, which may be measured either with respect to a plane, a line or a point. This can be illustrated by reference to the cube, which possesses twelve faces, of which the adjacent ones are at 90° to one another. Each face is described as a hexahedron. If a cube is cut into two symmetrical halves, one half will be the mirror-image of the other; the plane of division is described as a plane of symmetry. The cube can be divided in this way in nine different directions: three planes of symmetry each bisecting four edges, as above, and six planes of symmetry each cutting opposite faces diagonally, from corner to corner.

Pairs of planes of symmetry intersect one another within the crystal along straight lines. Each of these lines of intersection forms an axis of symmetry. Three of these axes of symmetry emerge through the centre point of opposite faces of the hexahedron, four axes pass through the opposite corners of the cube while six axes pass through the centre points of opposite pairs of edges. If the cube is rotated about any one of the three like axes, it is found to assume the same position in space four times in a revolution of 360°. It is therefore described as an axis of four-fold symmetry. Similarly, each of the four like axes is one of three-fold symmetry and each of the six like axes is of two-fold symmetry. All the axes intersect at the centre of symmetry. The complete symmetry of this form of cube may be summarised as follows:

$$
\begin{array}{rl}
9 & \text{planes of symmetry} \\
3 & \text{four-fold axes of symmetry} \\
4 & \text{three-fold axes of symmetry} \\
6 & \text{two-fold axes of symmetry} \\
\underline{1} & \text{centre of symmetry} \\
23 & \text{elements of symmetry}
\end{array}
$$

Crystal Forms

The crystal faces in each system have their own particular names. In the cubic system, the principal faces are those of the two forms known as the hexahedron and the octahedron. When a mineral crystallises in a characteristic form this is described as its habit. Thus diamond, in the cubic system, has an octahedral habit since it crystallises in this form rather than as a hexahedron. Diagrams of the various ways crystals form, and thus the systems in which they are classified, appear on pages 16–21.

When a crystal in a rock formation is dissolved away by an invading solution and replaced by another crystal substance, the latter – still showing the external form of the first crystal – is known as a pseudomorph. A compact crystal aggregate, such as occurs in the formation of calcareous stalactites and stalagmites, is termed massive. Chalcedony consists of minute crystals of quartz and is described as cryptocrystalline (Greek: *kryptos*, hidden).

Various Crystal Properties

Twinning is a property which many crystals possess. The simplest form of twinning occurs when two crystals grow together; the plane separating the two is described as the twinning plane. The twin axis passes through the centre of each twin, at right angles to the twinning plane. In spinel, for example, rotating one twin through 180° about the twin axis produces a complete octahedron. When a crystal is built up of numerous twins, it is said to exhibit repeated twinning; albite feldspar, with its lamellae, is an example of repeated twinning.

The property, which many crystals possess, of splitting in one or more directions parallel to crystal faces, is known as cleavage. Quartz, for example, has no cleavage, but fluorspar and diamond both cleave in directions parallel to the faces of the octahedron. Parting occurs when twinned crystals split along the twinning plane. When a crystal breaks along any plane other than that of cleavage, this is described as its fracture. Thus, quartz possesses a curving or conchoidal fracture; other types of fracture are said to be uneven, even, etc.

Crystal Structure

The alchemists, the 'scientists' of medieval times, described the very smallest part of a substance by the Greek word atom, a word which has become part of the phraseology of modern science.

Atoms of the same kind, when linked together, form simple chemical substances, known as elements. Some of these elements exist in nature in the form, for instance, of gold and silver, carbon and copper. But most of the earth's substances are chemical compounds, in which atoms of different kinds are bound together to form minerals. In a chemical formula, the ratio of the atoms of the various constituents is given; that of corundum, Al_2O_3, possessing two atoms of aluminium for every three atoms of oxygen.

At the centre of the atom are the protons and they, with the neutrons, constitute the nucleus. The number of protons in an atom is constant, specific and unique for every element, and provides the atomic number of that element. The protons have a positive electrical charge while the neutrons have no charge. The electrons, which lie outside the nucleus, and which correspond in number with the protons for the particular atom, bear a negative charge. The force of attraction between ions – electrically charged atoms – causes them to unite according to specific laws. When they assume solid form they have become crystals.

Different minerals can have identical chemical compositions. Thus Carbon (C) can crystallise both as diamond and as graphite. These two minerals are therefore called dimorphous (Greek, *di*, two; *morphe*, form). Anatase, brookite and rutile are examples of trimorphous minerals, that is, a substance that can crystallise as three different minerals. The ability of a chemical substance to crystallise into more than one mineral is termed polymorphism (Greek, *poly*, many; *morphe*, form). Elements with similar properties can replace one another in some crystal structures. This property is called isomorphism, or isomorphous substitution. The garnet and feldspar groups both form isomorphous series.

Minerals are classified according to their chemical composition, as the following examples indicate:

elements (diamond, graphite, gold, silver)
sulphides (pyrites, marcasite)
fluorides (fluorite)

CUBIC
Holohedral

cube
(hexahedron)
6 square sides

octahedron,
8 equilateral
triangles

rhombododecahedron,
12 rhombs

pyramidal cube,
tetrahexahedron
(24 isosceles
triangles)

CUBIC
Combined forms

cube and octahedron

octahedron
and dodecahedron

octahedron
cube
dodecahedron

pyramidal
cube and
cube

CUBIC
Lower classes and twins

pyritohedron
pentagonal dodecahedron,
12 pentagons

pyrites cube,
pyritohedral
faces, coarse
striations

diploid or dyakis-
dodecahedron

pyramidal octahedron
trisoctahedron,
24 triangles

trapezohedron,
24 trapezia

hexoctahedron,
48 triangles

octahedron
and trisoctahedron

dodecahedron and
trapezohedron

cube with 6
hexoctahedral
faces at each
corner

tetrahedron,
4 triangles

penetration
cube twins

octahedral
twins

octahedron
showing twin plane

17

TETRAGONAL

square
prism and base

ditetragonal
prism and base

double pyramid,
bipyramid

prism with pyramidal
terminations

HEXAGONAL

bases or
basal pinacoids

hexagonal
prism with base

12-sided prism
with base

TETRAGONAL

rhombohedron

scalenohedron

trigonal
bipyramid

trigonal prism
with pyramids

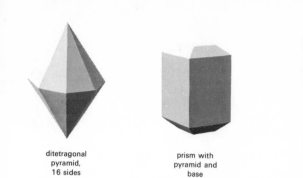

ditetragonal
pyramid,
16 sides

prism with
pyramid and
base

sphenoid,
defined by 4
triangles

hexagonal
bipyramid

dihexagonal
bipyramid

prism with basis
and various
pyramidal faces

prism,
pyramids,
base

trigonal prism
with pyramidal
faces

left-handed quartz

right-handed quartz

RHOMBIC

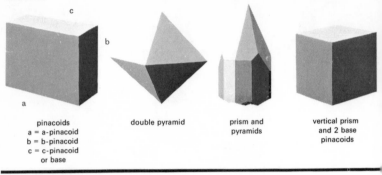

pinacoids
a = a-pinacoid
b = b-pinacoid
c = c-pinacoid
or base

double pyramid

prism and
pyramids

vertical prism
and 2 base
pinacoids

MONOCLINIC

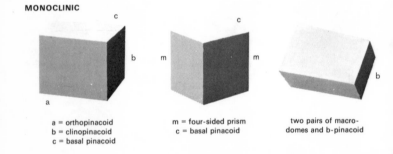

a = orthopinacoid
b = clinopinacoid
c = basal pinacoid

m = four-sided prism
c = basal pinacoid

two pairs of macro-
domes and b-pinacoid

TRICLINIC

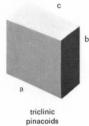  

triclinic
pinacoids

prisms, pinacoids
domes and pyramids

prism with
pyramidal and
pinacoid termination

prisms, domes
and pyramids

two pairs of transverse
domes and b-pinacoid

two pairs of
longitudinal domes
and a-pinacoid

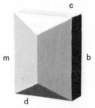

combination of prism (m),
transverse domes (d)
and b- and c-pinacoids

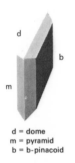

d = dome
m = pyramid
b = b-pinacoid

swallowtail
twins

carlsbad
penetration twins

carlsbad
contact twins

albite crystal

albite twins

albite, repeated
(lamellar) twinning

oxides (quartz, corundum, haematite, rutile)

carbonates (calcite, rhodochrosite, aragonite, malachite)

borates (colemanite)

sulphates (celestine, anglesite, gypsum)

phosphates (apatite, lazulite, amblygonite)

silicates (feldspar, rhodonite, beryl, garnet, peridot)

There are various simple tests by means of which these can be identified. Carbonates, for example, effervesce when in contact with dilute hydrochloric acid.

The surface hardness of crystals varies and can be classified according to Moh's scale of hardness (p. 47). All crystals can be identified by chemical or optical tests; the latter are more favoured by gemmologists since they do not damage the surfaces of crystals.

4 EXTRACTION OF GEMSTONES

The means of extracting riches from the earth vary considerably, from the most primitive manual operations to the most advanced mining techniques.

Probably the most sophisticated of all methods of extraction are those used in the great diamond mines of South Africa. First, roads are built, watercourses diverted, great reservoirs created, workers' accommodation and workshops erected and expensive equipment procured. Then miners may take several years to make an open pit. When an open mine can no longer be worked, shafts are sunk outside the diamond-bearing field and galleries are pushed forward level by level towards the centre where the diamond-bearing earth – kimberlite – is blasted away. Trains of tip wagons run from the mine to lifts which bring up the material, this is then passed through crushers and separators, leaving a concentrate of stones. These are taken by conveyor belt through many different sorting plants, each related to the particular properties of the materials to be separated. Thus the relatively high specific gravity of diamonds causes them to fall to the bottom of tanks, while the lighter stones can be skimmed off. In other cases, extracts from the mines are passed over vibrating tables or belts smeared with vaseline to which only diamonds adhere, other stones being washed away. Sometimes concentrates are X-rayed to make the diamonds fluoresce, photocells then identify the diamonds.

Where diamonds rest on ancient raised beaches, long since covered by many feet of desert sand, special bulldozers are used to remove the sand. Huge lorries remove the overburden, leaving the raised beach, in many cases as hard as concrete, to be broken up and transported by electric railways to plants where it is crushed, separated and sorted.

In the extensive areas of countryside between these gigantic engineering sites there may still be a few river diggings where watercourses once deposited the heaviest of the stones they carried. What was once a river valley may now be a hilltop. Holes are dug and the gravel is screened and put into a sieve, which, dipped in water and skilfully swirled, concentrates stones with high specific gravity in the centre.

Mining usually only starts after geologists have found a promising deposit. Indeed, the solitary prospector is being increasingly superseded by teams of highly skilled geologists with their sophisticated surveying methods. But it may not be worthwhile to employ mining engineers for a highly mechanised operation; thousands of mines and quarries are worked by only a handful of men.

How a deposit is exploited depends greatly on the rock's hardness. Poorly compacted or cemented rocks, such as clay and gravel, can easily be dug, but as the depth of a pit increases, hoisting apparatus must be installed to bring up the rubble. Ruby mines in Burma are worked in this manner, and ingenious flushing systems carry water to the washing flumes. Finally, when the material is in little baskets, the rubies can be distinguished from other small stones and separated from them on the basis of colour. In Sri Lanka (Ceylon) the gem-containing gravel, illam, is brought up from river beds or from water-filled pits and the contents separated manually in much the same way.

Blasting is necessary for opencast mining in hard rock, but this may spoil gems. When a pegmatite dike is quarried for pure feldspar and quartz intended for technical and chemical purposes, gem collectors may be allowed to remove crystals of smoky quartz, aquamarine, tourmaline and other minerals embedded in the walls of the mine. If there are many stones suitable for polishing, the owner may make a small incidental profit, but it is rarely worthwhile. Even in soft earth gems must be concentrated for organised mining to be economic.

In Colombia, where emeralds occur in soft rocks, cliffs are carefully terraced to find and remove the profitable green gems.

In Brazil, hydraulic mining is practised.

Hillsides of poorly consolidated material are washed by cascades of water from long-nozzled hoses. Then the sludge is scooped up and washed to isolate valuable stones.

In New Mexico, turquoises were formerly extracted by lighting fires at the base of limestone cliffs, then spraying the heated rock face with water until it cracked and collapsed and the turquoises could be extracted from the rubble. Ancient stories from Khorassan, in Persia, relate how horsemen with slings made the turquoises fall from crumbling slopes. Now, more prosaically, they are removed by means of passages dug horizontally into the cliffs.

In Australia, fissures are examined for opals by candlelight at night. Electric lighting is not suitable for this purpose. Similarly, ancient accounts report the nocturnal gem hunts on St John Island in the Red Sea, where the dazzling sunlight made it impossible to distinguish peridots from their surroundings during the day. Only towards sundown did their gleam make them visible. Nocturnal prospecting is now more popular than ever. Amateur American 'rock hounds' use ultra-violet lamps to reveal fluorescent minerals such as those containing uranium which emits a strong green light.

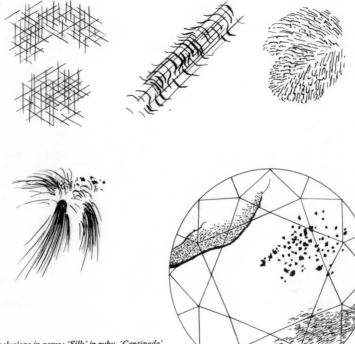

Inclusions in gems: 'Silk' in ruby. 'Centipede' in moonstone. 'Butterfly wings' or 'finger prints' in Sri Lanka sapphire. 'Ponytails' in demantoid. 'Piqués' in a diamond.

5 PHYSICAL PROPERTIES OF GEMS

To be precious, a stone must have a beautiful or interesting appearance, although other conditions may apply, as in the case of amulets or souvenirs worn for psychological reasons. Colour, transparency, lustre, the ability to refract light, visible inclusions and external form all combine to effect appearance.

There may be different varieties of a mineral (green and red tourmaline and tourmaline cat's-eye; Columbian and Indian emerald; moss agate and bloodstone jasper), and the same substance can occur both as a precious stone and as an ordinary variety (precious opal and common opal; gem diamond and industrial diamond; sapphire, ruby and emery).

Colour and Transparency

Colour is perceived with the eye when light falls on an object. The white light of the sun is composed of various colours, each with its own wave length. If an opaque object reflects the same amount of each colour, it appears white; if transparent, it looks colourless. If an object absorbs all the light, it is perceived as black. If, however, only part of the light is reflected, but the proportions of each colour in that light are equal, the object looks grey.

A precious stone will generally absorb some colours more than others, and it is the particular light that strikes the viewer's eye that indicates the stone's colour. White, grey and black are termed neutral colours. The colours of the spectrum from red to blue and purple are termed hues. If a colour is mixed with an increasing quantity of white, it becomes progressively lighter. Red becomes pink and is finally perceived as white with a slight tint. A bright yellow turns light yellow, pale yellow, and eventually a tinted white. If, instead, an increasing amount of black is added, any colour darkens and eventually becomes black.

In addition to the innumerable gradations between colours, such as greenish-yellow, yellowish-green, green, blue-green, there are dark and light tints and many shades of grey. It is therefore difficult to give a precise description of colour, even more so since the human eye can apparently perceive up to one million nuances of colour. Some gems are monochrome, others polychrome or variegated.

Some substances are so clear or transparent that even writing can be deciphered through them. Transparent stones are generally more highly prized than the opaque stones, which are so defined if light cannot shine through a slice of the mineral ground to a thickness of 0.04 mm. If some light is transmitted, but it is impossible to see clearly through a stone, the stone is termed translucent. Both transparency and translucency can be impaired by inclusions, and clarity often has a decisive influence on the value of stones, particularly diamonds.

Lustre

Some of the beauty of a stone depends on the brilliance of its surface and interior. Whether strong or weak, reflection from a surface is termed lustre. When light strikes a stone after passing through air, it is refracted, and the greater the refraction, the more the stone shines, as more light is reflected from the interior. Lustre is best seen on a smooth surface. This is the main reason why rough precious stones are polished. If the surface is left rough, the numerous small ridges merely reflect the light in many different directions. Smooth surfaces display three types of lustre: metallic, adamantine and vitreous, but these merge into one another.

Metallic lustre, which occurs in opaque materials, such as gold, silver and haematite, appears when the refractive index (see p. 52) is more than 2.5. Sub-metallic is the term used to describe a lustre such as that seen in columbite (611) which approaches metallic lustre.

Adamantine lustre occurs in precious stones, like diamond and zinc blende (sphalerite), with a refractive index of 1.9–2.5. Stones, such as corundum or zircon, which register an index between *c.* 1.7–2.1 are usually termed sub-adamantine.

Vitreous lustre (glass, rock crystal, peridot) occurs in most precious stones, the appropriate refractive index being 1.3 (that of water) to 1.8.

The various terms describing reflection from uneven surfaces – greasy, resinous, waxy (as in soapstone, amber and turquoise respectively) – describe the appearance of the surface in a self-evident way. Pearly sheen, in such stones as pearl, talc and amazonite, describes the appearance of surfaces on which very thin layers overlap, as with pearls, and the cleavage faces of many crystals. Silky sheen can be observed in fibrous materials, like tiger's eye, satin spar of gypsum or calcite and several types of wood, and resembles the reflection from close-set parallel, silken threads. This phenomenon is not only seen as a surface lustre but often mingles with the reflection from deeper-seated fibres.

Special Light Phenomena

Needle-like, parallel crystals or cavities which reflect light may be enclosed in a precious stone. If the stone is polished into a hemisphere, with the base set parallel to the length of the needles, the dome of the hemisphere acts as a convex lens. Each tiny needle becomes a gleaming point at the apex of the dome, and together all the points of light form a gleaming streak which moves with the light as it passes across the stone. This reflective phenomenon is termed chatoyancy, or cat's eye effect.

When the crystal needles lie parallel in three directions, the cabochon – a hemispherical polished stone – exhibits three streaks of light intersecting at a central point, to form a six-pointed star. This phenomenon is termed asterism or star effect. Star sapphire, star beryl and star almandine are only three of the many stones which can produce asterism. Four- and twelve-pointed stars also occur.

Moonstones display a mobile gleam which is not as sharp as chatoyancy, it is due to reflections from the stone's innumerable thin plates or twin crystals. There are also chatoyant moonstones and moonstones exhibiting asterism. In moonstone feldspar the sheen is termed adularescence, while the play of colour in the variety of feldspar

known as labradorite is called labradorescence, and is similarly ascribed to the lamellar (plate-like) structure of the mineral.

Glittering reflections from integral plates or flakes of mica or other very small crystals are called aventurescence. They appear in aventurine quartz and in aventurine feldspar (sunstone) and in the artificial product, aventurine glass or 'goldstone'. Both adularescence and aventurescence are commonly referred to as 'schiller lustres'.

Pearls not only display sheen but light is also reflected from layers beneath the transparent 'pearl skin'. Owing to interference, this light from the pearl is of a delicate hue, sometimes pale pink. Light is also reflected from layers beneath the surface of opals in approximately the same way, and because of interference this light has a milky or pearly appearance termed opalescence (a similar effect may be produced in opal glass). This opalescence should not be confused with the vivid play of colour inside genuine opals, which change colour constantly when turned this way and that, some containing all the colours of the spectrum from red to blue, others only those from green to blue. This play of colour is apparently caused by the passage of light between the closely set spheres which comprise the structure of opals.

Iridescence is a phenomenon produced by reflection from air-filled cracks in a stone such as iris quartz.

Inclusions

The appearance of a stone is often greatly influenced by the inclusion of extraneous crystals and other foreign bodies, by hollow spaces caused by cleavages and by negative crystals (cavities bounded by crystal faces). These optical impediments may affect the appearance of the stone superficially or deeply, and reflections from inclusions may render stones particularly attractive and valuable (see p. 24).

If the clarity of a diamond is blurred, the inclusions are termed piqués (French *piqué*, pricked). Expressions such as 'feather', 'cloud' and 'carbon' are merely descriptive terms. Rubies and other types of corundum may contain inclusions which resemble finely woven material, and for this reason have been termed silk. Corundums and other stones may contain cracks which have 'healed', and under magnification they present a net-like appearance variously described as 'fingerprints' or 'butterfly wings'. Plant-like crystalline inclusions are termed dendrites (Greek *dendron*, tree); those occurring in agate and opal may resemble ferns or moss, hence the terms moss agate, moss opal. While a crystal is growing, material of differing colours may be introduced and the growth lines can then develop intercalated bands, as in banded agate. These bands may take an irregular course, from which comes the term fortification agate. Or they may form concentric rings, hence peacock-eye malachite and eye-agate. When a 'ghost crystal' (caused by a temporary halt in growth or by a change in environment) can be seen within a rock crystal, it is termed 'phantom quartz'.

The golden specks in lapis lazuli are inclusions of foreign crystals (pyrites), while snowflake obsidian contains spherulites (spherical foreign crystals). White specks in some varieties of green nephrite are albite, a type of feldspar. *Flèches d'amour* (French, love-darts) in quartz may be hair-like sparkling crystals of rutile, while 'centipede' is a term for fractures inside moonstones. Needless to say there is no real silk in rubies and there are no genuine centipedes in moonstones. Only amber may contain inclusions which are real fragments of plants and animals, such as mosquitos, green-flies, spiders and even centipedes. (Amber is sometimes quite white because of multitudinous, air-filled cavities. It is then called bone amber.)

External Form

Handsome crystal forms occurring in nature are frequently used for settings (434, 462, 530, 627). A stone may also be singled out as a gem because of its distinctive natural form, such as the cross-shaped staurolite (605). Minerals which have lined rock cavities are occasionally found in unusual shapes resembling animals or human beings. Similarly, obsidian is found in tear-like forms (Apache tears, 100), and meerschaum sometimes resembles sculptures. Pearls may occur in shapes described as *poires* (French, pears), *boutons* (French, buttons), wing and monster pearls. However, minerals are usually shaped by ingenious polishing.

Corundum showing how the orientation of rutile needles produce (above) chatoyancy and (left) asterism.

6 THE GEM TRADE

Marketing methods for gems vary tremendously, mining companies fashion and market their own stones, or stones may change hands many times before reaching the stone cutter. Many rough stones are sold at auctions, such as those held at Idar-Oberstein in West Germany, in Japan cultured pearls are auctioned at regular intervals. But more and more international gem dealers are visiting the mining areas themselves, relying on valuable local contacts not only for information about available stones, but for the price negotiations, which are notoriously protracted and tough in the East, where the trading is considered an exciting sport.

Carat

While less valuable rough stones are sold by the kilogramme or even by the ton, expensive stones are sold by the carat. A karat is a standard of quality in gold (156–175), whereas a carat when applied to gems is a unit of weight equivalent to 0.2 grammes (200 milligrammes). Thus an 18 carat gem is a stone that weighs 3.6 grammes, while a piece of 18 karat gold may be any weight, 18 karat merely denoting that 18/24 (750 per thousand) of the weight is pure gold (the rest being an alloy). Unfortunately, the distinguishing use of 'karat' for gold and 'carat' for gems is not sufficiently consistent to be helpful.

The term carat or karat (Greek, *keration*), derives from the small fruit kernel of the locust or the carob tree (*Ceratonia siliqua*) which was once used as a measure of weight for gold, gems and certain valuable chemicals. As there are several species of carob tree, presumably there were definite rules for the selection of seeds as weights, but still the carat weight seems to have varied, nor was the situation improved by metal weights, which might vary by at least $\frac{1}{8}$ on either side of the 200 mg now recognised as standard. The metric carat of 200 mg was adopted by a convention in Paris in 1907 but was not immediately used by all traders, so specifications of the carat weight of diamonds and other stones before *c.* 1907–14 are based on the local, and not the metric, carat.

A carat is now divided into hundredths or points. The weight is given to two decimal places and for trade purposes this is not corrected even when the third decimal is 5 or more; for scientific purposes, however, more decimal places are necessary.

A grain or granule (latin, *granum*) is an ancient unit of weight, equivalent to the weight of a well-ripened, dry grain of wheat from the middle of the ear. The term grain is sometimes used in the gem trade and always for Oriental pearls of a certain size. There are 4 grains to a carat (1 grain = 50 mg) and in the pearl trade the grain weight is given to two decimal places without correction.

In Burma, Thailand and India, traders still use a unit of weight called the rati, which is strictly a seed from the abrus bush (*Abrus precatorius*). These seeds are known by Europeans as a jequirity bean or crab's eyes, being purplish-red with a black spot and containing a powerful poison (abrine). They are also used as ornaments, strung and worn as necklaces. In Japan, the unit of weight for cultured pearls is the momme, corresponding to 18.75 carats, though this has now been abandoned officially.

From Roman times, perhaps even earlier, the unit of weight for gold was the ounce (Latin, *uncia*). English-speaking countries in particular have used the ounce Troy of 31.10 gr, not to be confused with the avoirdupois ounce of 28.35 gr. But now there is increasing use of metric weights for gold and other metals.

Locust bean or carob seeds – probably the origin of the carat (half life size).

Special gold and carat balances, usually protected in glass cases, are used for weighing gold and gems respectively. The weights used for gold go down to $\frac{1}{10}$ gr or less and for carats they are as small as $\frac{1}{100}$ carat. However, such exact and sensitive balances are gradually being replaced by electronic balances which, on an illuminated scale, can instantly show the weight of a stone to hundredths of a carat or in milligrammes.

Measurement

When a stone is set in a piece of jewellery it may be necessary to estimate its weight using a diamond gauge. The simplest variety is fitted with holes of various sizes of carat, so that the hole which corresponds closest to the size of the diamond gives a rough idea of its weight. More accurate tests can be made by measuring the height, length and breadth of a diamond with a Moe gauge or Leveridge gauge and then tracing the approximate carat weight in the appropriate tables.

These diamond gauges are also useful when stones are sold by weight rather than dimension, such as many cabochons and all agates, and other semi-transparent to opaque stones of various cuts. With these the term 'addition millimetre' is used to signify length plus breadth. Thus, in an oval or rectangular stone 18 mm long and 13 mm wide, the two sides together measure 31 addition millimetres.

Gem Dealing

A collection of stones which are all cut to exactly the same size is said to be calibrated. Expensive calibrated stones, such as rubies, suitable for eternity rings are sold by the carat, not by size, while cheaper stones are usually sold according to the price of a single stone or more likely a hundred stones. Single stones, normally sold on the basis of cost per carat, are sometimes quoted at an inclusive price to eliminate the need for calculation.

A buyer must be familiar with the particular terms of purchase, whether it is by weight or measurement, at a given quoted carat price or inclusive price. Large collections of stones, such as an assortment of coloured sapphires, are sometimes offered at a lot price at so much a carat, when a buyer who only requires half the lot can select which half he wants, once the contents have been divided. But if a buyer only wants a few specific stones from the lot he may have to pay a premium of 50%, having most probably picked out the most valuable stones, leaving the seller to receive a lower price per carat for the remainder of the lot.

In the trade each lot of stones is kept in a parcel, consisting of paper sheets folded in a special way. Diamond parcels are usually lined with light-blue paper, emerald parcels with red cotton wool, opal parcels with black cotton wool or lining paper; all intended to provide the jewels with a flattering background.

The trade in cut and uncut stones takes place within a complicated international network in which there is keen competition between dealers, whose profits depend largely on favourable purchases. In some countries diamond exchanges, and in West Germany a general gem exchange at Idar-Oberstein, act as intermediaries between the trade and dealers, so helping to concentrate supply and demand and thus accelerate and facilitate trade, while exerting a constant and strict control.

Cutting and Polishing

The task of a lapidary is to shape a stone so as to emphasise its finest features of colour, transparency, lustre, light phenomena and refraction, but with the minimum loss of weight.

To judge from the pierced garnet crystals discovered among their household goods, the Bohemian lake-dwellers were clearly equal to the painstaking task of drilling hard stone, possibly using emery or crushed garnet powder. Garnet is not uniformly hard, so that powdered garnet could prove abrasive to another garnet. It was known at a very early stage that a hard stone could wear down a less hard stone and that garnet or corundum could cut rock crystal.

However, rock crystal and other minerals were not cut into symmetrical facets in antiquity, the preference was for smooth stones, some engraved for use as seals. It was not until the late Gothic period that faceted transparent gems were introduced.

TYPES OF CUT

STEP CUT. Step cut facets are all parallel to the girdle.

  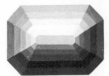

From above   From the side   From below

Step cut (mostly over 3mm)

Triangle   Square (two step)   Octagon or Emerald Cut   Trapezoid (Keystone)

Rhomb (Lozenge)   Pentagon   Hexagon

Step cut of small stones (mostly from 1–3mm)

Baguette   Tapered Baguette   Square   Single cut or 8/8
Top view   Side view   From below

Rounded step cut

Rounded step cut   Oval step cut   Drop step cut   Navette
or marquise   Cushion
step

STELLATE CUT

Round Brilliant Cut

Modified brilliant cut

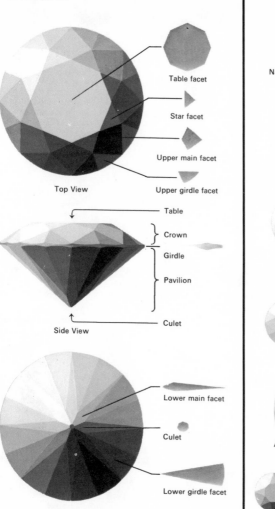

Table facet

Star facet

Upper main facet

Upper girdle facet

Top View

Table

Crown

Girdle

Pavilion

Culet

Side View

Lower main facet

Culet

Lower girdle facet

From Below

Navette (marquise)

Pear shape

Heart

Oval

Antique brilliant

Swiss cut

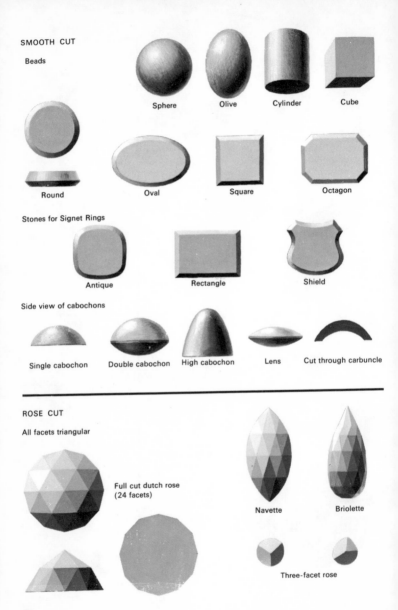

SMOOTH CUT

Beads

Sphere

Olive

Cylinder

Cube

Round

Oval

Square

Octagon

Stones for Signet Rings

Antique

Rectangle

Shield

Side view of cabochons

Single cabochon

Double cabochon

High cabochon

Lens

Cut through carbuncle

ROSE CUT

All facets triangular

Full cut dutch rose
(24 facets)

Navette

Briolette

Three-facet rose

32

SCISSOR CUT

From above

From the side

From below

MIXED CUT

From above

Antwerp rose (12 facets)
Step and rose cut

From the side

From below

Native cut

Chrysoprase cut
Cabochon with girdle
facets

Paronen cut star is mirrored
through the circular facets

Brilliant and step cut

Chessboard from above
and from the side.

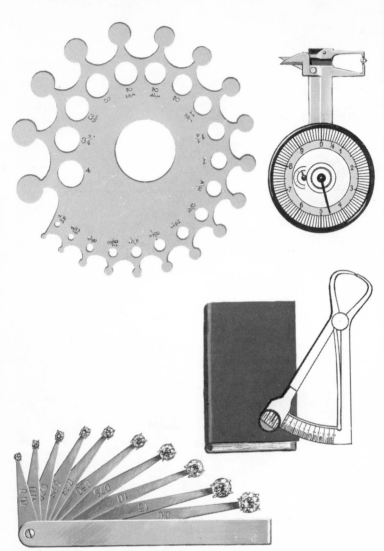

Four different kinds of diamond gauge. Top left *an aperture gauge*, right *a slide gauge.* Below *Moe's diamond gauge and a book of tables. Bottom left a diamond comparison gauge with synthetic spinels.*

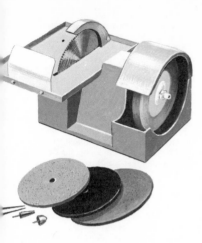

Basic gem preparation kit for the amateur, consisting of saw, polishing discs and other items.

Drum or tumble polisher. Large quantities of baroque stones (colour plates 217, 244) can be tumble-polished in rotating drums to which abrasives are added and then polishing agents.

Diamond cutting was apparently introduced in the fifteenth century, supposedly by a certain Louis van Bergen (or Berquen) of Antwerp. The rose cut for diamonds was presumably known by the time of Cardinal Mazarin, since he placed orders for them; he may in fact have invented the cut himself, but evidence is slim, as it is also for the claim that Vicenzio Peruzzi in the seventeenth century invented the brilliant cut. Diamond cutting is covered under Diamond (124–155), see also illustrations on pages 166–67.

The technique of grinding consists in fining down or smoothing a stone with the mechanical aid of abrasives. Powdered garnet, corundum (emery) or artificial agents such as carborundum are used, but with its unique hardness powdered diamond is preferred, since it enables the work to be more exact and rapid, although it is expensive. Powdered abrasives are employed for drilling, sawing and grinding with vertically or horizontally rotating wheels. Especially fine powders are used for polishing, or smoothing out and buffing a surface, also special polishing agents which are softer than the stone being prepared, for example, pumice, tripoli, crushed haematite mixed to form a soft mass (jeweller's rouge). Under high magnification, a rough surface can be seen to consist of many small peaks. After polishing with soft agents these flow out and form a layer, the Beilby layer, which is rendered partly or wholly amorphous or crystalline by the friction. Certain stones, such as diamonds, do not produce a Beilby layer, so the surface must be ground smooth with very fine-grained diamond powder.

Before grinding, some stones are sawn into shape, others are trimmed with a light hammer, others with good cleavage in the desired direction are split with a chisel set into a previously prepared small incision which is then tapped.

Cutting is an extremely complicated and specialised skill which entails, among other tasks, shaping cabochons and other smooth items, also called agate cutting (see illustration p. 32), faceting, drilling and engraving. When rock crystal is faceted for mounting in rings, already sawn blocks are further sawn into slabs and divided into squares, which are then ground with a vertical wheel to give the stones a rectangular shape with a carinate base. Then the stones are firmly fixed on dop sticks before they pass to the facet cutter. The stones have to be cemented on the dop sticks in several positions as the work progresses. Before polishing the rock crystal looks rough and whitish but once polished each facet is like a clear window revealing the stone's limpid interior. Naturally, mass production enables a lapidary to be even more efficient, but generally, for economic reasons, lapidaries specialise, grinding beads for necklaces, or fashioning small bowls and ash-trays, making signets and smooth convex cabochons.

Faceting too has its specialists, especially in transparent stones, such as tourmaline, which must be aligned according to their crystal structure to bring out the best colour. Nevertheless, lapidaries are normally conversant with all aspects of the process, with the possible exception of engraving which requires a particular talent for lettering and figuring.

With a diamond-set drill an engraver cuts letters, monograms, coats of arms, and even portraits in signets, and scribes or engraves small figures, such as cameos, in agate, amethyst and other stones.

The gem cutter's workshop may also house experts in other processes, for stones are often heated to give a more even distribution of colour or to change the colour. Thus, topaz can become pink, smoky quartz or amethyst can turn golden to red-golden, brownish-green tourmaline can become emerald green and brown tansanite blue. Porous stones may be steeped in various baths to absorb dyes. Grey agate, for example, absorbs carbohydrate, is then treated with sulphuric acid and heated, ending up as coal-black onyx. Most agates are coloured artificially, quite an acceptable practice provided the colour is fast and the trade description correct. Agate does not, after all, become chrysoprase when it has been coloured green and it should be sold as artificially green agate. But an agate which has been coloured blue remains a blue agate to the trade.

Setting

Setting entails fitting and securing a gem in metal or another material. The illustrations on p. 37 show the various types of setting arranged in the order in which they are described below.

If a stone is sunk into the metal itself, some of which is then pushed inwards over the stone to hold it, this is termed incrustation. If a special mount is constructed to hold the stone, it is called a setting.

The box is an old type of single stone setting consisting of sides raised on a base, which may be square or rectangular, or the sides may be bent to follow the contour of the stone. Flat signet stones are usually mounted so the top of the setting edge is forced over the oblique facet (or bezel) and often ground down, lapped level with the table facet of the stone, to produce a flush setting. A circular box, also known as a collet setting, is made from a piece of chenier tubing; the stone is fitted into the box or tube, and secured by the sides which are pressed down over the girdle.

In a coronet setting a curved metal strip which forms a slightly conical housing for the stone is used and the metal is sawn away until a small crown is shaped. A small ring support may be soldered beneath the coronet and the inside of the spires incised to form a ledge to support the stone, with the top of the grips bent slightly over the stone. Similarly, a box setting may be turned into a claw setting. Often the sides of settings are patterned with pierced work (gallery) or engraved imitation piercing.

Claws are not confined to independent settings, they may also be sawn or filed out of an integral piece of metal, like the gypsy ring and the crown setting in which the claws are produced by paring down the metal between the projected claws. This was once a popular setting for rose cut diamonds.

The square setting is used for one or more small stones, held in place by tiny grains or rounded metal chips worked up from the surrounding metal. To make a stone, for instance a small diamond, appear larger, distinct sloping cuts are made towards the stone from the framing edge, which in this and other settings is impressed with a beaded pattern called millegrains (French, a thousand grains) by means of a special graining wheel.

SETTINGS

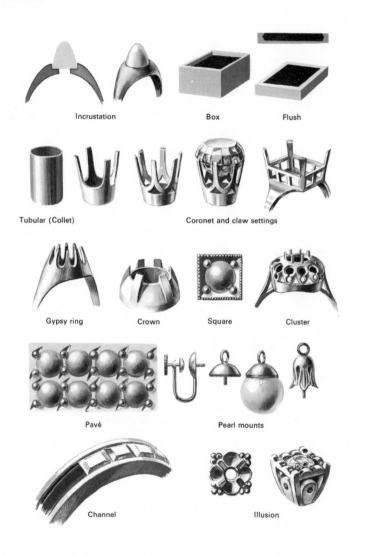

Incrustation

Box

Flush

Tubular (Collet)

Coronet and claw settings

Gypsy ring

Crown

Square

Cluster

Pavé

Pearl mounts

Channel

Illusion

Several single stone settings may be soldered in a row or other patterns, such as round a larger centre stone or in a cluster setting. The latter can also be constructed as one large setting, the side of which is a collet delicately cut into gallery and claws, the top being one round plate with sockets for satellites and centre stone and additional claws for the centre stone.

Many closely set stones or half-pearls held by grains form the *pavé* (French, paved) setting, which may partly cover a piece of jewellery. Extra grains and millegrain edges produce an ornamental illusion of many more stones.

Mounts for half-drilled pearls, for ear-screws and pendants, often consist of a bowl-shaped or floral base with a central peg on which the pearl is cemented. This form of mount is also used for round stones and drops.

Eternity rings and other pieces made up of a single row of stones may consist of several single stone settings soldered together, or two circular bands may be bridged to accommodate square stones tightly between them in a channel setting. Round stones may be mounted *à jour* (French, light) in a solid ring shank in millegrained square settings or in a close row; in this latter only the border edges can be millegrained (136) so the sides are engraved to resemble open-work.

Deceptive settings with extra grains and brightly burnished metal parts to create an optical illusion of a larger centre stone are termed illusion or mirage settings.

There are also closed settings, which have a base. A metal foil may be placed under a transparent stone, silvery for colourless stones, coloured for others, to enhance the brilliance and colour or even to change the colour. Thus, rock crystal is back-foiled in old jewellery, book clasps, vinaigrettes and church silver to give the illusion of amethyst, ruby and emerald. Contemporary closed settings are similarly deceptive: what seems to be an emerald with the appropriate refraction and inclusions may well be a colourless beryl set on a green metal foil by the tricky process of foiling in which the setting must be perfectly tight, as the slightest dampness mists the foil and destroys the effect.

Dirt and grease on the underside of a stone reduce the brilliance, so normally a small hole is bored in the base of a setting of transparent stones to facilitate cleaning.

Many jewellery expressions vary from one workshop to another. Thus the common term bezel, strictly denoting the oblique facet sloping down from the table facet to the girdle of a stone, or the metal rim or setting edge after it has been bent obliquely to hold a stone, is wrongly used for a whole setting or part of a setting such as a support or ledge.

Names of Stones and Gems

The names of some stones are thousands of years old, whereas other newly discovered minerals have not yet been named.

Ancient names such as opal (Sanskrit, *upala*), sapphire (Hebrew, *sappir*), jasper (Syrian, *aspu*; Hebrew, *yashpeh*), and agate (after the ancient, and now untraceable, Sicilian river Achates) all presumably come from the Middle and Far East.

Ancient names of definite Greek origin include diamond (Greek, *adamas*, unbreakable), malachite (from the word for mallow plant), chrysolite (literally golden stone). Many Greek names end in *-lithos*, stone, and the suffix *-lite* is still used when naming new minerals.

From Latin we have lapis lazuli (Latin, *lapis*, stone; Arabic *lazuli*, azure). Latin adjectival suffixes such as *-ianus*, *-inus* and *-itus* were used throughout ancient and medieval times, but gradually the adjectives were turned into substantives: *beryllus aquamarinus* (beryl resembling seawater) became aquamarine, *hyacinthus rubinus* (red hyacinth corundum) became ruby. *Lapis nephriticus* (kidney stone) became nephrite. Later, and this practice persists today, Latin endings were added to place names, for example, brazilianite from Brazil (Brazilian stone); to personal names, such as prehnite after Colonel Prehn; or as suffixes to a special property, like mirabilite, from *sal mirabile*, miraculous salt. The suffix -ine gives names such as kornerupine (from the personal name Kornerup); with -ian, vesuvian (of the mountain Vesuvius), which sometimes, as vesuvianite, has yet another adjectival suffix.

The traditional expressions of German miners give us words such as quartz (German, *Quarz*), and blende, (German, *Blende*) as in zinc blende. The ending -spar is cognate with the German *-spat* and related to the German verb, *spalten*, to split, and is applied to minerals such as feldspar and fluorspar which have distinct cleavage properties.

It should also be remembered that names have shifted from stone to stone. In old texts a sapphire was an opaque blue stone flecked with gold – the stone today called lapis lazuli. Similarly, names like hyacinth, chrysolite, topaz and jasper (which once referred to a transparent stone) have first been given to one, then another, mineral. The science of mineralogy has helped to organise nomenclature, but unsuitable names are unfortunately still perpetuated. Within the gem trade a stone is sometimes given the name of a better known and more coveted one. In this book such misnomers and the trade names of synthetic stones have been deleted.

A synthetic stone should bear the word 'synthetic' followed by the name of the reproduced mineral or chemical composition, for example, 'synthetic ruby' or 'synthetic strontium titanate'. Today all newly created names of minerals have to be submitted to an international commission of mineralogists for approval and registration according to strict criteria. Besides names approved by this commission there are many other trade names of gems and their varieties from times past. A stone must not be called by a name belonging to another gem, nor by a name very like another. The mineralogical name should be used. Other names are allowed if no objection can be raised on ethical grounds. Names must not be ambiguous, and unnecessary names should be avoided. There are, however, instances where it is useful for a variety to have its own name as well as the mineral name. Thus, when zoisite, which was previously known only as an almost opaque green or red mineral, was recently found in Tanzania in a transparent form from blue to mauve, it seemed preferable to call the variety tansanite, to differentiate it from the older known form of the mineral.

It would certainly be easier if gems had the same name in every language. But even when the names are similar, spelling may differ. The Greek k sound (kappa) becomes c in Latin and appears as either c or k in modern languages. Greek *chi* becomes *ch* in some languages, but k in others. The s sound occurs as s, c or z. The h sound disappears in some languages, so that aspirated r may be written rh and sometimes r on its own, just as h can be dropped from the prefix of a word (essonite, hessonite). Suffixes particularly differ. It has been suggested that the first four letters of the name of a stone should be the same in all languages, but this rule can only be observed with regard to the more recent names.

7 GEMS IN ANCIENT TIMES

Our knowledge of civilisation indicates that people wore jewels from a very early date, indeed we know more of ancient jewels than clothing. But why certain stones were chosen as amulets and jewellery in prehistoric times is unknown. Long before the ancient cultures of Babylon, Assyria and the Indus valley, men revered stones, as archaeologists have discovered from excavations of graves and settlements containing gems, though the finds are too sparse to show which stones were used first. Among the oldest known jewels are amber, nephrite, garnet, rock crystal, amethyst, serpentine, emerald, pearl, coral and the shells of mussels, snails and sea urchins. Others may well have been used, though they have not survived or have not yet been discovered.

Cylindrical seals from Babylon and neighbouring areas were carved so that they could be rolled over clay tablets and impress the design. Pierced lengthwise they could be worn on a string round the neck or wrist. The earliest of these seals are seven thousand years old. The materials initially comprised soft varieties of soapstone (steatite), serpentine and marble, and later lapis lazuli, haematite, amazonite, jasper and various rock crystals. Cylindrical seals and other seals indicate that glyptography (Greek, *glyphein*, carve) – the art of carving characters and figures on precious stones – is

Egyptian intaglio carving with grazing stag.

many thousands of years old. The Egyptians carved intaglios and scarabs (amulets depicting the sacred beetle) engraved with hieroglyphs on the underside, from carnelian, chalcedony, green jasper, lapis lazuli, amazonite, amethyst, turquoise, emerald and ruby. Carved seals from Minoan Crete are also known. The Greeks and Romans perfected the art of glyptography in the so-called antique gems. These are precious stones such as amethyst, rock crystal, carnelian and jasper, carved to depict idols, mythological scenes, portraits, animals and other characters. The delicate workmanship is admirable, both artistically and technically, especially as the magnifying glass had not then been invented.

The setting of jewels in gold and silver had already begun in the Early Bronze Age, by which time the skills of mining and forging were well-known. The history of gems is thus largely linked with that of the decorative arts and handicrafts, both sacred and profane.

In early times the magical properties supposed to exist in gems were no doubt an important reason for wearing them. The American mineralogist and gemmologist, George F. Kunz (1856–1932), points out that this belief may have been the original reason for the wearing of jewels. Throughout the Middle Ages it was believed that gems possessed supernatural powers. There were, of course, sceptics, but as late as the seventeenth century doctors prescribed medicines based on jewels, and used precious stones for external therapy. Stones were thought to protect their owners from misfortune, some were viewed as antidotes to poison or as prophylactics, some were said to prevent fires. Others would apparently enhance a person's desirability, warm husbands' flagging love for their wives, elicit favour from princes, bring fortunes or render their wearers invisible. Some could shine in the darkness, prevent plague, heal wounds, stop bleeding or cure the sick.

In medical practice gems were applied to affected spots and stones rubbed around them. Vulnerary salves of crushed jewels were prepared and medicines containing crushed pearls, sapphire (lapis lazuli), malachite and stibnite (antimony) were particularly sought after. A medicine called *opiata antimelancholica* was used in a case of depression with compulsion neurosis in 1667. The prescription contained, in addition to opium, *confectio de hyacintho*, medicated emerald, pearls and red coral.

Gems were regarded as particularly effective amulets (Latin, *amuletum*, a protection against sickness and evil). The word charm, or a lucky pendant comes, via French, from the Latin *carmen*, lyric poetry or magic formula. A mascot is a figure or object which brings luck, a word dating from the First World War in France in the form *mascotte*, related, perhaps, to *mascaron*, meaning a grotesque figure or witch. Similarly a talisman is an object with magical protective powers derived from the Arabic *tilsam*, in turn a derivative of the Greek infinitive *telein*, to consecrate or sanctify. The words are almost interchangeable, but a mascot is usually in the form of a figure.

Not surprisingly, a stone's colour could suggest some of the ideas concerning its miraculous powers. Thus, red stones were said to encourage the blood circulation or stop bleeding, or might even cause an enemy to bleed to death. Stones the colour of the sea were supposed to help sailors and voyagers. Green stones would make fields and gardens turn green. But these beliefs also followed mythological lines, revolving around religious faith and the power of the heavenly bodies. The blue of the sapphire apparently gave the eyes superhuman strength to gaze into the blue sky and see the future. Blue was also symbolically linked with the goddess of love and the virgin deity, both of whom were protected by blue stones. Gold, being the colour of the sun, was connected with the summer months and autumn leaves. Gold and red were colours of the sun-god, whose powers rested with the lion. This god's representative, the king, bore a lion's emblem on his shield and the red ruby was the ruler's stone. Purple stones, reminiscent of wine, enabled one to drink without unpleasant consequence. In the Christian church purple and then amethyst became the colours of the bishops,

later superseded by celestial blue and sapphire, the bishop's stone.

In Egypt jasper, lapis lazuli, feldspar, carnelian, serpentine and other stones have been found, each engraved with an extract from the Book of the Dead. These may well have been considered sacred to the deity invoked in the pertinent extract, and since the gods in many instances were identified with heavenly bodies this could well be ancient evidence of the supposed connection between gems and the stars.

Gems and Symbols

Various old sources describe to which signs of the zodiac particular stones belonged, but as stones were sometimes catalogued according to the zodiac and sometimes according to the months, the results varied greatly. But, traditionally, amethyst belongs to February and topaz to November. After much research it is now generally agreed that the following stones are associated with each month:

January	garnet
February	amethyst
March	aquamarine, bloodstone jasper
April	diamond, rock crystal
May	emerald, chrysoprase
June	pearl, moonstone
July	ruby, carnelian
August	peridot, sardonyx, jade
September	sapphire, lapis lazuli, coral
October	opal, tourmaline
November	topaz, amber, citrine
December	turquoise

Precious stones and certain metals have also come to symbolise anniversaries. Thus, the notion of silver and golden wedding anniversaries dates from about the first half of the nineteenth century. In the following list the stones for some of these anniversaries are given:

Wedding Anniversaries
1. Rose wedding or Beryl wedding (pink beryl, aquamarine) or paper wedding
2. Crystal wedding or cotton wedding
3. Chrysoprase wedding or leather wedding
4. Moonstone wedding or silk wedding

5. Carnelian wedding or wood wedding
 6. Peridot wedding or sugar wedding
 7. Coral wedding or wool wedding
 8. Opal wedding or clay wedding
 9. Citrine wedding or willow wedding
10. Turquoise wedding or tin wedding
11. Garnet wedding
12. Amethyst wedding or linen wedding
13. Agate wedding
14. Ivory wedding or lace wedding
15. Topaz wedding
25. Silver wedding
30. Pearl wedding, pearl jubilee
35. Jade wedding
40. Ruby wedding, ruby jubilee
45. Sapphire wedding
50. Golden wedding, golden jubilee

55. Emerald wedding
60. Diamond wedding, diamond jubilee

An akrostikon was an ancient Greek verse in which the initial letters of each line made a word. In the eighteenth and nineteenth centuries such acrostic poems became fashionable again, so much so that jewellery was made up with rows or circles of stones, the initials of which formed a word. Queen Ingrid, Queen Mother of Denmark (b.1910) has two such bracelets which belonged to Josephine Beauharnais (1763–1814), later Napoleon's empress. The initials of the stones in the bracelets form the Christian names of Josephine's two children Eugene and Hortense.

Ornaments described as jewellery are generally classified as:

Head ornaments the most regal of which is, of course, the crown. A diadem or tiara (290) is a half-circlet studded with jewels, wider above the forehead than at the sides. Hair-combs (45) and slides (65) may be simple or richly ornamented. There are many types of fillet and frontlet and the latter may be covered with stones or decorated with a pendant pearl.

Ear ornaments (323) may be secured with a clip or screw (56), or a hoop or screw fixed in a perforation through the ear. Sometimes the hoop encircles the ear and occasionally hair and ear ornaments are combined. Ear ornaments come in many styles, rosettes, movable pendants suspended from it, or a combination of the two (563) are popular.

Facial ornaments are most usually spectacles and lorgnettes which are sometimes embellished. In India the women of some castes wear a diamond set in the wing of the nose.

Neck ornaments come in varied styles. Necklaces (158) often consist of one or more chains of gold or other material and necklets are solid, collar-shaped ornaments. Strung necklaces are made of many different materials, including pearls (9) or stone beads (641). Strung with ornaments all the same size a necklace is called uniform, if the ornaments vary in size it is described as graduated. Some necklaces hug the neck, others hang loosely in various lengths; some have a clasp (768) which can vary from a simple hook and eye to an intricate box lock, which is a fine piece of jewellery in itself. Pendants can be attached to necklaces (522). There are many different types, including medallions which consist of two lockets to hold portraits or souvenirs (49). Further types of neck ornament include the collar of an order and the chain of office worn by mayors and chairmen of societies.

Hand ornaments normally consist of finger-rings (154), but the whole hand has been known to be covered like a glove. Rings were once worn on all the fingers and all the finger joints. A plain, smooth, metal ring (163) is used as a wedding or an engagement ring in some countries, but most rings have a table, or head, with shoulders forming a transition to the shank (633). This table or head is variously designed, made of gold alone (172) or mounted with stones. A ring with only one stone, particularly a diamond, is called a solitaire (140) and used in many countries as an engagement ring. A twisted ring (378) is an incomplete circle set with one or more stones in which the ends of the shanks finish parallel and obliquely to each other. Rings with stones in alignment (347) usually have an uneven number of stones mounted on the shanks. One with stones of a uniform size in full circle is called an alliance or eternity ring (136, 343), it signifies an alliance between two people and is therefore also used as a wedding ring. When the stones form a semi-circle the result is a half-hoop ring. If the ring's crown bears a large stone framed by smaller ones it is sometimes called a cluster ring (314). There are also gentlemen's rings with signet stones (212), countless fancy or dress rings (384), as well as those bearing the insignia of various associations and offices.

Arm ornaments are chiefly bracelets (160, 176, 185, 192, 773) and bangles in various forms and patterns. They encircle either the wrist or other parts of the arm. A bracelet is jointed (94), while a bangle or armlet may be a rigid open circle slipped over the hand (464), or closed with a hinge or clasp (166); it may also be made of wire or formed into a wide cuff. Many bracelets bear charms, either for luck or as souvenirs, such as a four-leaf-clover, hearts (253) or a miniature Eastern pagoda. Finally, a fine, decorative, wrist-watch (138) may be considered as a kindred form of arm ornament.

Body jewellery, such as studded belts and navel ornaments, is rarely used, although in some countries, anklets and toe-rings are used to adorn the legs and feet.

Jewellery worn on clothing comes in great variety. It is attached by a pin, clip or screw set at the back of the ornament. Pins and brooches (187, 386) are made in every conceivable shape to be worn on dress, collar, belt, scarf, hat or turban. There are belts made of gold in the form of chains or plates set with gems, and ornamental buckles for belts and shoes. An agraffe is a special clasp which holds clothing together, and buttons may be carved from stone or made of gold and silver. Men's cuff links (299) are made of similar materials.

Decorations (393), medals and badges belong to a special category of ornaments, as do devotional ornaments. Crosses (190), rosaries and many other religious items are usually fashioned in gold.

Accessories denote those small requisites carried in people's pockets or handbags, such as combs, lipstick cases (191), powder compacts (47), cigar and cigarette cases, cigar prickers and cutters, cigarette holders (95), pocket knives, pillboxes (165), snuffboxes (48), lighters (174), gentlemen's watches with chatelaines (173), boxes for saccharine tablets (193) and other small boxes (261).

The use which has been made of gems in the whole range of jewellery is ingenious in the extreme, and every conceivable natural and artificial material has been utilised (see 800–820).

Care of Jewellery
More jewellery is lost through carelessness than by theft. Rings are left in toilet rooms; brooches are left on coats in cloakrooms; jewellery is left on dresses and shirts sent for cleaning. Jewel casks may be stolen if left in hotel rooms instead of being deposited in the hotel safe. In cold weather or when bathing in the sea, the fingers shrink and rings may slip off.

In the jewel cask each piece needs a separate compartment or silk bag, to prevent the items from scratching each other; deep wounds in pearls, marred opals, and diamonds scarred by other diamonds are sad results. Emeralds, topazes and kunzites are brittle and should be handled with the utmost care.

Diamonds, rubies and sapphires regain their lustre when gently cleaned in tepid water, but a hard brush may distort the delicate claw settings and cause the loss of a stone. Pearls (except imitation ones) may be dipped in alcohol and wiped with a damp chamois leather. But pearls and porous stones like opals, corals and turquoises will be ruined in strong cleaning agents. Blue turquoise may turn green from cosmetic cream. Likewise, pearls darken if they absorb hair lacquer. Gems may crack if suddenly placed on a cold plate. Turquoise, amethyst and rose quartz may fade if exposed to strong sun light. Opal may crack in the heat if not protected by a thin film of olive oil.

Jewels should be regularly checked by a jeweller, and should be insured with an all-risk jewellery policy.

9 GEMMOLOGY

Gemmology, the science of gems, is not merely concerned with minerals, which include the majority of gems, but covers jewellery materials in the widest sense, including such organic substances as pearls and coral, as well as synthetic and imitation substances. The specialist English term gemmologist, with its cognates, gemmology and gemmological, was apparently coined in the late nineteenth century, and all these terms derive from the Latin *gemma*, a jewel, which originally meant flower-bud.

Not all the stones used in jewellery are genuine. Treated, or artificially changed stones, synthetics and pure imitations can be supremely deceptive. Thus, with the development of mass-produced synthetic stones and large-scale cultivation of pearls in Japan, it has become imperative to intensify gemmological research in techniques of identification.

The science was well established, with specialist books about it, at least 2500 years ago. One particularly rare book about it is *Peri Lithon* (On Stones) written about 315 BC by the Greek philosopher and naturalist, Theophrastos (372–287 BC), the heir of Aristotle (384–322 BC). Aristotle's own *Book of Stones* has now proved to be a much later 'pseudo-Aristotelian' work. In Volume 37 of his *Natural History*, Pliny the Elder (AD 23–70), quotes about forty authors from the ancient world, on the subject of gems, thus providing a valuable source-book about the ancients' knowledge of stones.

Although gemmology is mainly a branch of mineralogy, it has been regarded as an independent science since the end of the eighteenth century. But before then the German physician, Georgius Agricola (Georg Bauer, 1494–1555), had suggested a logical system for the classification of minerals on the basis of well-defined chemical criteria. However, it was not until 1735 that the first complete system of classification of minerals (and animals and plants), *Systema Natura*, was published, by the Swedish naturalist, Carolus Linnaeus (Carl von Linné, 1707–78). Then, in 1758, Linnaeus' compatriot, Axel Fredric von Cronstedt (1722–65), suggested, in *Försök till Mineralogi* (Attempt at Mineralogy), a classification system based on chemistry. Another Swede, the chemist Jöns Jakob Berzelius (1779–1848), actually established a classification system for minerals on a chemical basis (1812) and introduced the chemical symbols.

In 1837, the American mineralogist, James Dwight Dana (1813–95) published his first *System of Mineralogy*, based on natural history. In 1854, however, in the fourth edition, he changed to a chemical system based largely, but not exclusively, on the principles of Cronstedt and Berzelius. Dana's system, which is still being updated, is an important foundation for modern mineralogy.

Mineralogy only developed gradually but it was a significant advance when in 1784 the learned French abbot, René Just Haüy (1743–1822), worked out the fundamental law of crystallography which earned him respect as the acclaimed father of crystallography and mineralogy. Similarly, the German geologist, Abraham Gottlob Werner (1750–1817) and his school have had a deep influence on mineralogy.

During this century the science has continued to expand. Many countries have established schools of gemmology and research centres for this science, as well as gemmological and lapidary societies.

Throughout the world, official research laboratories and gemmological societies have been established, publishing specialist journals which help to increase the knowledge of gems, report the latest methods of testing gems and detection of synthetic and forged stones.

However, such laboratories and the tests they use require expert knowledge and highly specialised and expensive equipment. The individual, amateur gemmologist must obviously rely on other means of identification. For him, the elimination method of determination, whereby exclusive characteristics distinguish one gem from another, is probably the best. The following equipment and tests will aid identification.

The Magnifying Glass

A specimen is first examined with the gemmologist's most important instrument, a magnifying glass or small jeweller's loupe, which has several lenses mounted on top of each other which can be swivelled in and out of a small casing. The glass most commonly used is a jeweller's lens which magnifies 10 times. Its spherical convex form must not distort the view of the specimen by spherical aberration, so an aplanatic lens is included in the mounting; nor should the glass reproduce incorrect colours in the specimen by the lens itself causing dispersion.

The lens is held close to the eye with one hand while the other brings the specimen into the sharpest possible focus, with the minimum of movement. All examination of stones must be done with adequate lighting.

Under magnification, the following conditions in a specimen can be defined: colour and distribution of colour, inclusions, fractures and cleavage, external scratches, polish, the sharpness of the facets' edges, the condition of the girdle and the join of a doublet. Dispersion too is more pronounced; an apparently strong lustre suggests a high refractive index, double refraction is sometimes also apparent under the $10 \times$ lens.

Tweezers

Tweezers are another important item of equipment for the gemmologist. Both snipe and flat tweezers are available as well as tweezers with slides to keep the specimen in position. But care must be taken, for too firm a grip with the tweezers can damage the girdle of even hard stones and can scratch soft stones such as fluorite and calcite.

Microscope

Much more efficient than a magnifying glass, a microscope needs several magnifications, starting from $10 \times$, to ensure a large visual field for the initial examination. It should be possible to rotate the stage plate on which the stone is placed, and the stone must be fixed in a rotating clamp so it can be lowered into a bowl of liquid (the immersion chamber). Good lighting is necessary and the microscope should have nicol prisms to polarise the light.

Hardness Tests

Hardness can best be defined as the ability to resist physical pressure, but it is necessary to state the sort of pressure intended. For purposes of mineralogy, a very simple hardness test was devised by Friedrich Mohs (1773–1839), a German mineralogist working in Austria. In this test, ten minerals were rated from 1 to 10 according to their hardness. This was determined by their ability to scratch softer minerals, or be themselves marked when forcefully scratched with a harder one. However, the scale is uneven; there is a big jump from diamond to corundum and very little difference between the minerals at the lower end of the scale, so it is useful only as a scale of relative, rather than absolute hardness. Since hardness is a directional property it can in some minerals vary according to the orientation of the crystals, but this is not usually significant, except in the spectacular instance of the mineral kyanite, which varies from $4\frac{1}{2}$ to 7 on Mohs' scale:

A modern diamond microscope with stereoscopic lighting from below and above; direct illumination and dark field; magnification 10 ×–45 ×; tweezers; can be fitted with measuring device for size of cut and with polaroid camera.

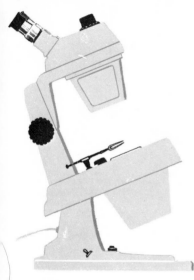

Mohs' scale of hardness
1. talc
2. gypsum
3. calcite
4. fluorite
5. apatite
6. orthoclase
7. quartz
8. topaz
9. corundum
10. diamond

Goldsmiths once believed that genuine stone could be distinguished from imitation with the use of a steel file. As this has a hardness of between 6 and 7 Mohs many good, but softer, stones were ruined when tested in this way. An ordinary knife has a hardness of 5–6 Mohs and stones with a hardness of 2 can be scratched with a finger nail.

It has been said that dust in the air contains sand or grains of quartz which can scratch stones with a hardness below 7 Mohs, making such stones unsuitable for use as jewels. However, it is only with a very high wind force that sand makes any impression on stones.

Streak Tests
The powder of some minerals has a characteristic colour which can be determined by scraping a little powder onto white paper. A clearer result, however, is obtained by drawing a line with the mineral across an unglazed porcelain plate or, better still, an unpolished agate plate (521). Streak tests are only used in identifying unpolished minerals with a metallic lustre, such as haematite which makes a red streak, and pyrites (iron pyrites) with its characteristic greenish-black to brownish-black streak. Streak tests are also used to assess the approximate karat of gold (503).

Electrical Properties
The word electricity comes from the Greek *electron*, amber. This is electrified by friction, attracting bits of paper, hair and dust. Tourmaline is electrified by rubbing or warming, and is positive at one end and negative at the other.

Magnetism
The mineral magnetite is attracted by a magnet, while ferrous minerals such as haematite and pyrites, containing a large quantity of iron, are not magnetic. However, it has been demonstrated that some ferrous gems lose weight when subjected to magnetic attraction. Even when a stone is placed in a balance on an insulating cork mat or stopper, strong magnetic action alters the equilibrium in the case of heamatite, some garnets (almandite, spessartite, demantoid and pyrope), rhodonite and rhodochrosite, epidote and peridot among others. This test is useful for distinguishing such singly-refractive stones as demantoid and green diamond.

Sensory Impressions
A stone's character is also perceptible in other ways. For example, meerschaum and topaz may feel particularly smooth to the

touch, while soapstone feels greasy. The texture of oriental and cultured pearls feels rough when they are rubbed against the edge of the front teeth, while wax pearls naturally feel waxy. Some people detect a peculiar sound when two pieces of jade are tapped against each other, a characteristic frequently used in oriental music. Topaz is said to cool the tongue and slake thirst, but none of the minerals which have a real taste, for instance halite which is salty, are used in jewellery, and few minerals which have a particular smell are used. When it burns, amber gives off a pleasant smell of incense, while scorodite (618) smells like garlic when it is heated. Plastic imitation stones, except acrylics which smell like perfume, emit a foul stench when heated or burned.

Specific Gravity or Density

Since different substances with the same volume do not have the same weight, a calculation is made of the ratio between weight and volume, namely specific weight density. Density can be calculated, theoretically, on the basis of a mineral's chemical composition, its atomic weight and the distance between the atoms in its make-up. In practice, density is usually expressed as grammes per cubic centimetre or as an abstract figure.

For the practical determination of density, or specific gravity, a famous principle is used, according to which a body in water loses the same weight as that of the water it displaces. Thus the weight of a body in the air is divided by the weight loss of the body when immersed in water, the resultant proportion being different for light and heavy metals. This law was formulated by the Greek scientist, Archimedes (c. 287–212 BC) to distinguish gold from base metals.

This method of discrimination by hydrostatic weighing (Greek, *hydro*, water, *statis*, weighing) is still used. In liquids of varying density, the 'heavy liquids', the relative buoyancy of a stone can be ascertained, that is, whether it floats on the surface, remains in suspension or sinks. A fairly accurate solution can be made up in which a stone neither floats on the surface nor sinks to the bottom but remains suspended, then, with the aid of a specific gravity indicator (a piece

Specific gravity or density test in a heavy liquid. The stone lighter than the liquid floats on the surface, the stone with the same density as the liquid is suspended, and the stone at the bottom has a higher density than the liquid. The most favoured liquids are: Clerici's solution (S.G. 4.25 and downwards); methylene iodide (S.G. 3.33); and bromoforme (S.G. 2.88); they can all be diluted to lower grades of density.

of glass or stone with a given density), or by measuring the liquid's refraction of light on a refractometer, the density of the solution and the stone can be traced in the appropriate table.

Sometimes merely the approximate density figure is sufficient to determine a stone. Thus, to ensure a piece of amber is not a plastic imitation, it should be placed with some genuine amber in a glass of water into which salt is stirred and dissolved until the genuine test amber rises. If the other piece remains at the bottom of the brine it is not amber.

Some mines have separation plants which use this method to isolate diamonds from lighter minerals. All the stones to be sorted are poured into a tank containing a heavy liquid or emulsion (colloid). The light stones are skimmed off and the heavy material with the diamonds is sluiced out at the bottom.

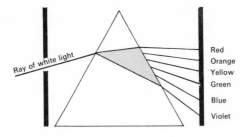

Red
Orange
Yellow
Green
Blue
Violet

The experiment made by Sir Isaac Newton in 1669 to show the dispersion of light. The glass prism disperses the white light into the colours of the spectrum.

Optical Properties

The English physicist and mathematician, Isaac Newton (1642–1727), passed sunlight through a glass prism onto a white screen where the light was broken into all the colours of the spectrum. In another experiment he showed that the coloured rays could be reconstituted as white light. The division of white light into coloured rays is called dispersion. The colours forming the visible spectrum are called the spectral colours, but the hues beyond violet and red are not visible.

Dispersion is generally characteristic of gems and shows most clearly when they are colourless. Green demantoid garnet shows stronger dispersion than diamond, but its colour veils the effect. Similarly, dispersion is less apparent in coloured than white diamonds. Synthetic rutile and strontium titanate have a very strong dispersive effect so that it is often possible to distinguish them from diamonds with the naked eye. Strass (lead glass) can superficially resemble a diamond because of its pronounced dispersion.

The spectrum of a gemstone can be observed through a spectroscope. There are hand spectroscopes through which daylight can be seen separated into colours. At the same time a series of black lines is visible. These are the Fraunhofer lines, named after the German physicist, Joseph Fraunhofer (1787–1826), who discovered them in 1814.

These dark line spectra are designated by letters B to G.

The dispersion of a gemstone is usually measured between B and G. As shown in the diagram of Newton's prism experiment, violet light bends more than red light. When measuring the refraction of a gemstone in red and in violet light the dispersion (B–G) will be the difference between the two.

If we pass white light through a gem or let the gem reflect it and observe the reflected light through a spectroscope, we see similar lines or even broad bands – absorption spectra – which stand out as stronger or weaker markings among the colours. There can also be bright lines – emission spectra. If the spectroscope is also provided with a wave-length scale the position of the lines can be exactly determined.

Many gems have very characteristic spectra which are a great help in identification and in distinguishing them from imitations. The density and refractive index of a Thai ruby and a garnet are very similar, but they are easily distinguished on the basis of their different spectra.

Various colour filters used to exclude or suppress certain colours are also based on absorption principles. More than one filter may be placed in the path of the rays. The filter most used by gemmologists is the Chelsea colour filter. Mounted like a magnifying glass, the filter almost exclusively permits red and green rays to pass through.

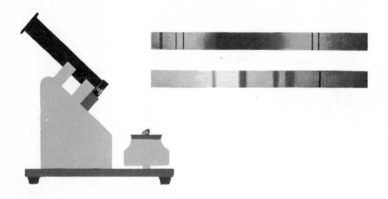

| Red | Orange | | Yellow | | Green | Blue | Indigo | Violet |

The position of the prominent Fraunhofer lines B to G in the solar spectrum. (A to H is the part of the spectrum perceptible to the human eye.)

Left: *Spectroscope.* Right, *two different gem spectra: ruby* (top) garnet (below), *but both stones may have the same colour.*

Emeralds look very red, as do synthetic stones, but most other green stones remain green or appear black. Demantoid garnet appears light reddish. Aquamarine becomes green or colourless; its imitation, synthetic spinel, alters from light-blue to reddish.

Light is emitted mainly by glowing materials such as incandescent metals and gases. These substances are then called luminous. Other substances are not visible until they have been struck by emitted light rays which are reflected or transmitted by them.

However, light can also be emitted from bodies which are not incandescent, especially where there is a change in wave-length, called luminescence (Latin, *lumen*, light or torch). Fluorescence, one form of luminescence, takes its name from fluorite (fluospar).

In 1852 the British physicist, George Gabriel Stokes (1819–1903), described how ultraviolet rays cause fluospar to glow in the dark, and he explained this phenomenon. Part of the energy from absorbed ultraviolet rays is apparently transformed into heat and the remaining energy is converted into visible rays of longer wave-length emitted from the mineral. Some substances are more strongly fluorescent than others, and this property is a useful aid for many purposes, including distinguishing synthetic from genuine gemstones. Fluorescence caused by X-rays helps to distinguish between oriental pearls, freshwater pearls and cultured pearls.

Fluorescence stops immediately irradiation ceases. In contrast, phosphorescence is a luminescent phenomenon wherein a sub-

Fluorescent lamp.

stance continues to glow after irradiation has ceased. Diamonds can phosphoresce after they have ceased to fluoresce. They can also emit light when rubbed across the grain of wood. This phenomenon is called triboluminescence (Greek, *tribos*, friction). When a substance is made to fluoresce by being heated, but without being raised to incandescent temperature, the phenomenon is called thermoluminescence (Greek, *thermo*, heat). Green fluorite (chlorophite) displays thermoluminescence but infra-red (heat) waves rather than ultraviolet waves produce the luminescence.

Reflection
When a ray of light strikes a gemstone it meets a substance which is optically denser and some light will be reflected. The actual quantity of reflected light depends on the penetrability of the gemstone. Greater deflection of the ray causes greater reflection from the gemstones. Lustre is a feature of reflection and stones which are very refractive will show a greater lustre from the reflective surface.

Reflection can also occur within a stone. When light penetrates a polished diamond it emerges either through posterior facets or is reflected back into the stone, the facets acting as mirrors. But since the light is

passing from a dense to a less dense medium all the light *may* be internally reflected, so that none actually emerges from the facets. Diamond, being very refractive, only permits light to escape if the light strikes the interior within a certain critical angle. If the light strikes a facet at an angle exceeding 24° 26′ it is reflected back entirely. The lower part of brilliant diamonds is cut at an angle of 40° 45′ so that every ray of light is reflected back into the crystal. The rays will be reflected through the top facets of the stone and intermingle with the surface lustre, producing brilliancy.

Absorption
Absorption of light by a substance determines its colour and transparency. If light is entirely absorbed the substance appears black; if equal quantities of all wave-lengths are absorbed, the substance will appear white or grey. If rays of certain wave-lengths are absorbed while rays of other wave-lengths pass through, selective absorption occurs and the stone acquires a hue.

Penetrability of a stone by light is termed transparency. (Degrees of transparency have been discussed on p. 25.) Transparency can also refer to penetrability by invisible rays. Some gemstones, like diamonds, can be penetrated by ultraviolet rays. Diamonds are also among those which can be penetrated by X-rays. An X-ray photograph (sciagram) shows lead glass, zircon and other substances containing metals as opaque, black objects, while diamonds are scarcely visible.

Refraction
That part of incident light which is not reflected but passes into a gemstone changes direction upon striking the interface. This bending is called refraction and most gemstones refract light to a varying degree, which is an important aid to identification.

In cubic crystals and amorphous substances the incident ray, after being refracted, continues as a single ray regardless of direction. Such substances are called singly refractive, or isotropic (Greek, *iso-*, the same; *tropos*, direction).

The Danish scientist, Rasmus Bartholin (1625–98), discovered in 1669 that the inci-

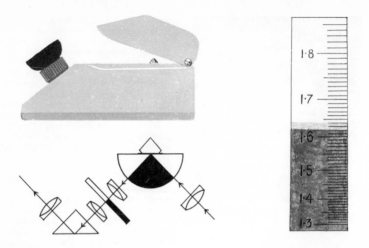

Refractometer. The path of the ray in the refractometer is based on total reflection. The reading is linked with the critical angle of the stone.

dent light ray is split, which is the reason objects seen through Iceland spar (calcite) appear double. We now call this phenomenon double refraction or anisotropy. All crystals except cubic crystals are anisotropic, but doubly refractive crystals are singly refractive along their optical axes. Crystals of the tetragonal, hexagonal and trigonal systems have only one optical axis; those belonging to the rhombic, monoclinic and triclinic systems have two such directions.

Velocity of Light
When a ray of light strikes the interface the light ray is retarded as well as refracted before it penetrates the stone. The reduction of the speed of light is proportional to the bending it undergoes. In air the velocity of light is almost 300,000 km per second. In obsidian, for example, the speed of light can be reduced to 200,000 km per second. The ratio between the velocity of light through air and through obsidian is $\frac{300,000}{200,000} = 1.50$, which is the refractive index, n, of obsidian. In diamond, the velocity of a ray of yellow light is reduced to *c.* 124,000 km per second,

yielding a refractive index of 2.417 with respect to yellow light. Violet light is refracted most strongly of all types of light (n = 2.465), while red light is refracted least (n = 2.407).

Measuring Refraction
The easiest way to measure refraction is with a refractometer. Excellent gem refractometers can be bought, but they measure refractive indices only up to *c.* 1.80 and measurement is precise only if the specimen has a facet. Measurements of cabochons are less reliable.

A gem refractometer operates on the principle of total reflection. A ray is directed from a lamp (preferably sodium) into the instrument. The light is refracted in an optically dense (highly refractive) hemispherical or prismatic glass. The stone to be measured is placed upon this glass and a fluid of high refractive index provides optical contact between specimen and glass. When a light ray strikes the stone some light penetrates it, but some is reflected through the glass. Because the critical angle for incident light striking different substances varies, the glass is divided into light and dark parts which differ according to the type of stone being studied. The light ray then passes through a transparent screen and is prismatically bent towards the eyepiece of the refractometer. Through the eyepiece the screen appears divided into light and dark portions at the junction of which the refractive index of the stone is indicated. If two edges of shadows appear, alternately or simultaneously, the stone is doubly refractive. If only one edge of a shadow appears the stone should be rotated to ascertain that there is no other reading.

There are other methods of determining a stone's refractive index, but they become highly complex and technical. Should testing with a refractometer be unsuccessful, a gemmological society will be able to give advice.

The Dichroscope

The dichroscope (formerly called the Haidinger loupe) was invented by Dr Wilhelm Karl Ritter von Haidinger (1795–1871), a Viennese mineralogist. Used to determine double refraction, it consists of a small tube with a cleavage rhomb of calcite (Iceland spar). The calcite exhibits such a high degree of double refraction that one can see two images clearly through it. At one end of the tube is an eyepiece; at the other there is a rectangular window. When the dichroscope is held up to the light there appear to be two windows as viewed through the eyepiece. A coloured stone is held in front of the window and rotated (or the instrument is rotated). The colour may change, but during the course of one rotation the same colour will reappear four times. This is because the ordinary and extraordinary rays in a doubly-refractive stone exhibit varying degrees of absorption. A ruby will appear carmine and yellowish-red; a sapphire will usually appear blue and a dirty yellow.

However, there are reservations to the use of the dichroscope: not all coloured, doubly-refractive stones are dichroic; a doubly-refractive stone is singly-refractive (isotropic) along an optical axis and must therefore be rotated; colourless stones show only one colour; stones which are scarcely transparent must be illuminated. When a stone shows two colours it *must* be doubly refractive, but stones which do not show two colours are *not* necessarily isotropic. The quality of light is also important when using the dichroscope. In reddish light, alexandrite will gradually show one green and two reds, but in bluish light it will show two greens and one red.

11 *COLLECTIONS OF GEMS AND MINERALS*

Stones have been collected since ancient times. Beneath the ruins of the ancient city of Ur, the archaeological museum of the Babylonian princess, Bel-Shalti-Nannar (*c.* 550 BC) has revealed a fine collection of stones, some already a couple of thousand years old in the sixth century BC. Collections of finger rings were started by the rulers and rich citizens of Rome. Julius Caesar had a particularly fine collection of intaglio and cameo gems.

Valuable royal collections of *objets d'art* and gifts from philanthropists form the nucleus of many museums and national collections. Mineralogical collections are usually grouped into rocks, fossils and minerals, the last classified according to chemistry and isomorphism with a special section for precious stones. Among public collections, the American one in the Smithsonian Institution, Washington, DC and that at the Natural History Museum (British Museum), London, are exceptional.

The amateur can exhibit the larger items of his collection on book shelves and in glass-fronted cases. The smaller specimens can be displayed in glass boxes, display, or compartment showcases and stored in stone papers. Good lighting is important; transparent stones look particularly well on a ground glass plate lit from below, while moss agates and other stones with fine inclusions are best illuminated from behind. Specimens with star and cat's eye effect are best if spotlighted. Fluorescent minerals and rocks can be displayed in a darkroom or merely a deep cupboard lined with black and equipped with ultraviolet lamps. Systematic records should be kept of each acquisition, with name, provenance and other relevant data, and a corresponding serial number attached to the specimen itself.

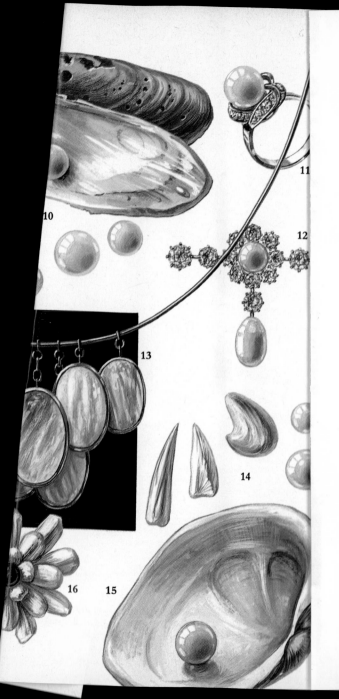

10

11

12

13

14

15

16

NOTE TO THE COLOUR PLATES

On the following pages are 820 illustrations of jewels, gems, precious stones, imitation stones and materials used in making jewellery. It is probably the first time that so many examples have appeared in one book. The majority of items are drawn to scale, only a very few are enlarged or reduced.

The examples of jewellery are mainly contemporary pieces. The emphasis has been on showing everyday items and not merely unique museum pieces. The provenance of examples is, however, less limited. Exotic as well as familiar pieces have been shown.

The order in which the pieces are presented is determined by their place in the crystal systems. Organic materials, such as pearl, shell, nautilus and coral, as well as fossils and amorphous rocks, are dealt with first. Then follow the cubic minerals (124–276), the tetragonal (277–308), the hexagonal and trigonal (309–544), the rhombic (545–627), the monoclinic (628–728) and finally triclinic minerals (729–762). The last pages show examples of pieces used for jewellery which are wholly or partly man-made, such as cultured pearls, synthetic stones and various imitations.

Freshwater pearls

1. Shell with blister pearls. 2. Oriental mother o[f] white pearls. 4. Coloured pearls. 5. Red pinna pe[arls] 8. Shell with pearl. 9. Necklace of graduated pea[rls]

Salt-water pearls

1. Shell with blister pearls. **2**. Oriental mother of pearl carved and engraved. **3**. Small white pearls. **4**. Coloured pearls. **5**. Red pinna pearl. **6**. Pearl droplet. **7**. Baroque pearl. **8**. Shell with pearl. **9**. Necklace of graduated pearls.

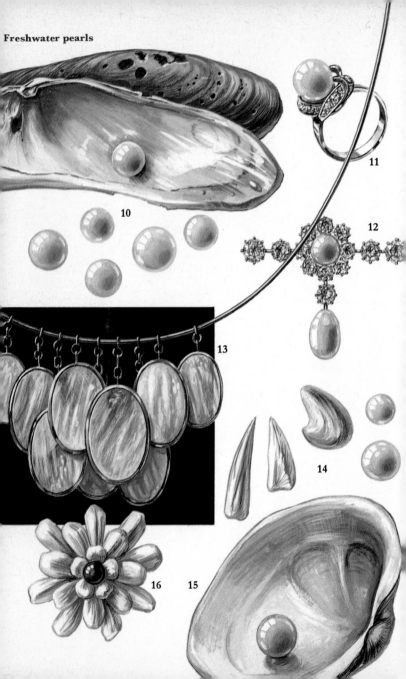

Freshwater pearls

10

11

12

13

14

15

16

COLOUR PLATES

NOTE TO THE COLOUR PLATES

On the following pages are 820 illustrations of jewels, gems, precious stones, imitation stones and materials used in making jewellery. It is probably the first time that so many examples have appeared in one book. The majority of items are drawn to scale, only a very few are enlarged or reduced.

The examples of jewellery are mainly contemporary pieces. The emphasis has been on showing everyday items and not merely unique museum pieces. The provenance of examples is, however, less limited. Exotic as well as familiar pieces have been shown.

The order in which the pieces are presented is determined by their place in the crystal systems. Organic materials, such as pearl, shell, nautilus and coral, as well as fossils and amorphous rocks, are dealt with first. Then follow the cubic minerals (124–276), the tetragonal (277–308), the hexagonal and trigonal (309–544), the rhombic (545–627), the monoclinic (628–728) and finally triclinic minerals (729–762). The last pages show examples of pieces used for jewellery which are wholly or partly man-made, such as cultured pearls, synthetic stones and various imitations.